The human mind plans the way, but the Lord directs the steps.

Proverbs 16:9 (NRSV)

The Journey: Missional Accountability is an excellent study guide to help congregations focus both on the mission aspect of their work and on "purpose over preference" being "at the heart of missional accountability." Jaye Johnson uses the three foundational elements of spiritual growth, leadership, and purpose to help churches have a clear understanding of missional accountability. He also includes great questions for congregations to bring their churches into missional alignment.

Dirk Elliott, Michigan Conference of The United Methodist Church

Great leaders are willing to sacrifice their personal preferences for the sake of the mission of their organization. Dr. Jaye Johnson uses the image of a road trip to describe the journey of healthy congregations toward the goal of joining God in redeeming the world. Clergy and laity alike will benefit from Johnson's conviction that by watching over one another in love, disciples of Jesus Christ unleash the power of the Holy Spirit to partner with God in developing passionate and adaptable leaders who are equipped to lead others on the Greatest Expedition of all: sharing Christ's love with the world.

Bishop Laurie Haller, Iowa & Dakotas Conferences of The United Methodist Church

Jaye Johnson is one of the most remarkable experts on missional leadership in the North American Christian context. A seasoned pastor, a clergy coach, and a guru around various assessments for leveraging more effective leadership, he has written an incisive text for pastors and congregational leadership teams who want to understand how to lead congregations through the murky cultural waters of North American in the 21st century. I commend this book with great enthusiasm!

Elmer M Colyer, University of Dubuque Theological Seminary

Dr. Johnson is gifted in making the complex accessible. He has the God-given ability to lead congregations & pastors in discovering and faithfully responding to God's purpose for their lives and ministries. In *The Journey: Missional Accountability*, Dr. Johnson has found a way to put his in-person abilities to the printed word. This book holds great potential for God to bless you, and through you, bless others.

Charliam Renner, Embarras River D.S. (Illinois Great Rivers Conference)

Reading this book reminds me of a colleague who teaches preaching and requires each student to have a title for their sermon. This colleague says the sermon title is a contract between the preacher and the listener to keep them focused on where they are headed together.

The Journey: Missional Accountability helps name that contract for leaders and their churches to accomplish more and celebrate the journey of getting there. So, buckle up for this Road Trip to strengthen your church (I mean, God's Church) and its ministry!

Phil Schroeder, Dunwoody (Georgia) UMC

THE JOURNEY:
MISSIONAL ACCOUNTABILITY

The Vehicle, Driver and Destination
of Your Congregation

Jaye Johnson

the greatest
EXPEDITION

THE JOURNEY:
MISSIONAL ACCOUNTABILITY

The Vehicle, Driver and Destination of Your Congregation

©2021 Jaye Johnson

books@marketsquarebooks.com
P.O. Box 23664   Knoxville, Tennessee 37933
ISBN: 978-1-950899-35-7

Printed and Bound in the United States of America
Cover Illustration & Book Design ©2021 Market Square Publishing, LLC
Publisher: Kevin Slimp
Editors: Kristin Lighter & Kay Kotan

Unless otherwise noted, scripture quotations are from

(NRSV)

This resource was commissioned as
one of many interconnected steps in the
journey of *The Greatest Expedition*.

EXPEDITION

GreatestExpedition.com

Table of Contents

Foreword

This resource was commissioned as one of many interconnected steps in the journey of *The Greatest Expedition*. While each step is important individually, we intentionally built the multi-step Essentials Pack and the Expansion Pack to provide a richer and fuller experience with the greatest potential for transformation and introducing more people to a relationship with Jesus Christ. For more information, visit GreatestExpedition.org.

However, we also recognize you may be exploring this resource apart from *The Greatest Expedition*. You might find yourself on a personal journey, a small group journey, or perhaps a church leadership team journey.

We are so glad you are on this journey!

As you take each step in your expedition, your Expedition Team will discover whether the ministry tools you will be exploring will be utilized only for the Expedition Team or if this expedition will be a congregational journey. Our hope and prayer is *The Greatest Expedition* is indeed a congregational journey, but if it proves to be a solo journey for just the Expedition Team, God will still do amazing things through your intentional exploration, discernment, and faithful next steps.

Regardless of how you came to discover *The Greatest Expedition,* it will pave the way to a new God-inspired expedition. Be brave and courageous on your journey through *The Greatest Expedition!*

Kay L Kotan, PCC
Director, *The Greatest Expedition*

INTRODUCTION
Traveling Styles

My wife and I have very different traveling styles. When traveling by car, Amy loves to stop often, look at roadside attractions, and have as much fun as possible along the way. For her, getting to our destination is half the fun. On the other hand, I prefer to stop as infrequently as possible. Better yet, let's fly. For me, traveling is a means to an end; for Amy, it is part of the journey.

Over the years, we have mostly found ways to negotiate these differences. Still, when about two-thirds of the way through a trip, the moment arrives when we must choose which of these styles will guide the rest of our journey. Will we push on to enjoy ourselves when we get there, or will we enjoy what we are doing now? When we travel and reach this point, my lovely wife typically gives in, lets me win, and takes a nap.

I suspect many of you might be smiling right now as you think about trips you have taken with loved ones. For readers participating in *The Greatest Expedition,* which is now about two-thirds of the way complete, your Expedition Team might be feeling some of the same tension. Some of you might be thinking, "Can't we just move this along and do what needs doing?" Others of you are enjoying the journey and are in no hurry to finish.

Before you move on, take a moment to reflect on these questions:

- Which type of traveler are you?

- How do you negotiate differences when you travel with others?

- Which type of traveler do you think each of your Expedition Team might be?

- How might this impact your expedition?

This resource on missional accountability will help your Expedition Team stay focused and negotiate differences. Practicing missional accountability will help you navigate the moments when some in your church want to stop at roadside attractions, and others want to "push on" as quickly as possible toward the goal. Don't tell my wife, but stopping along the way is sometimes necessary and can even be fun. Other times, it is critical for the expedition to keep moving as quickly as possible.

CHAPTER ONE
Sudden Stops

Most of the time, during travel, sudden or unplanned stops are not good.

One summer, my family was rolling down the I-70 in Colorado in our F-350 at full highway speed, pulling our 28-foot camper behind us. Everyone else was sleeping when suddenly, we came up over a hill to find that traffic was at a dead stop! In moments like that, time seems to slow down, and the speed of thinking seems to accelerate exponentially. My first thought was, "We can't hit that car!" (Actually, that was my second thought. My first thought would not be appropriate to write here.) An appraisal of the situation quickly followed those earliest thoughts:

- Do I have time to stop?

- If I slam on the brakes, will I jack-knife the trailer?

- What about the shoulder?

- Is the ditch an option?

- What about the people behind me?

- Thank God my family is buckled in!

I immediately decided to hit the brakes hard, including the button on my truck that engages the engine brake. While slowing down, I hit the hazard flashers to warn others behind us of our sudden, unplanned stop. Thankfully, we stopped with feet to spare. While I was relieved that I stopped safely, just like that, everyone in the truck was wide awake! Whether traveling or in the church or the expedition, a sudden stop can be a wake-up call insisting that we think and act quickly. These moments provide opportunities for correction and action, which are at the heart of missional accountability.

One such moment occurred for me as we were crammed into the basement of a small, rural, family-run church building, talking about the congregation's future. I kept asking, "What would God want from us?" Interestingly, the answers that came back were not about what God wanted, but what they wanted. I asked again, "What would God want from us?"

I could feel the frustration level growing in the room, especially in one woman. After The fourth or fifth time I asked, "What would God want from us?" she slammed her hand down on the table, causing the bad church-basement coffee to spill from our Styrofoam cups, and exclaimed, "This is our church! WHAT DOES GOD HAVE TO DO WITH IT?"

It was a sudden, unplanned stop. I typically like to move expeditiously to fill silences, but I allowed those words to hang in the air for an uncomfortable amount of time. "Well," she said, looking down at the floor, "that is not what I meant." However, I think it was what she meant. She named precisely what most of the people from that church were feeling at that moment. What God was calling them to do had not registered in their collective discernment process.

That memorable meeting was one of my

first encounters with a church that needed missional accountability. Years later, author and church consultant Doug Anderson taught me that 90 percent of US churches are in decline, and only 10 percent are growing. The primary difference between them is not music, theology, size, location, culture, Pastor, denomination, or programming; the difference is that the growing 10 percent have leaders (clergy and laity alike) inclined to sacrifice their preferences – what they want – for God's purpose. Purpose over preference is at the heart of missional accountability. Choosing purpose in the heat of the moment is not regularly, if ever, comfortable, but it is essential.

CHAPTER TWO
Where Are We Headed?

Churches that excel at the art of missional accountability tend to be healthy and vital, while those that neglect this discipline find themselves steeply declining. This look into missional accountability will begin by defining "missional accountability." Missional accountability is the process of looking over one another and the church in love in order to stay focused on joining God in redeeming the world. There are three foundational elements of missional accountability: spiritual growth, leadership, and purpose. Missional accountability thrives in the dynamic interaction and overlap of these three key elements.

Think of spiritual growth as the vehicle for missional accountability of a congregation, leadership as the driver, and purpose as the destination. All three of these are topics worthy of exploration. You will be reading or will have already read some resources from your Essential Pack on some of these topics, but when combined, we see something unique and critical to the vitality of communities of faith.

Missional accountability is not about criticism or punishment, but rather directional correction leading to encouragement, support, and a clear picture of reality. Churches that resist missional accountability find themselves in steep decline as they lose focus on why and for whom the church exists: "This is our church! What does God have to do with it?" These rapidly declining churches are seeking to fulfill their own preferences rather than God's purpose.

While we find struggling churches in different contexts, theological backgrounds, sizes, and cultures, declining congregations have one thing in common: There is a palpable lack of focus on what God desires. They have collectively ceased seeking God's plan for their congregations and communities. Conversely, all thriving churches have leaders fearlessly living in God's purpose, both as individuals and collectively as a congregation. They are drivers willing to do what is required to steer the church toward that purpose, even when it may be uncomfortable or cause others to become disgruntled.

Concentrating on the mission is complicated when individuals are dismayed, but it is essential. Missional accountability is not a quick fix; it is often a slow and painstaking process requiring frequent evaluation and adjustment. This assessment and correction must take place inside the leader and must overflow to impact the congregation. Healthy congregations and expeditions have high-quality leaders who do not fear accountability, but welcome it. They see it as either affirmation that they are faithfully living God's intention or as an opportunity for a course correction. Before continuing this expedition, we need to pack our bags with the items we will need along the way. In other words, we need to define some terms so that we have a shared understanding and language for discussing this expedition toward missional accountability.

CHAPTER THREE
Defining Terms

When I was writing my doctoral dissertation, my advisor used to say, "You must define your terms. Just because you know what you mean by those words does not mean that others will." Because I took that lesson to heart (and just in case Dr. Martin is reading), this section will define my terms.

What do I mean by missional accountability?

Missional accountability is looking over one another and the church in love to make sure that together we stay focused on joining God in redeeming the world. Missional accountability keeps the leaders and the expedition or church motivated and supported as they grow in their relationship to God, one another, and the mission. Missional accountability is what helps expeditions and churches keep, as Stephen Covey says, "the main thing the main thing."[1]

Missional accountability blossoms in the dynamic intersection where spiritual growth, leadership, and purpose converge. But before we can examine what that dynamic interaction looks like, we need to break down and define the words "mission" and "accountability" individually.

Mission

I was teaching a class at the University of Dubuque Theological Seminary, and we were discussing mission. As a pastor, consultant, and leadership coach, I indicated that mission is about discovering God's intention and letting that objective guide our movements and decisions. Mission is what enables congregations to focus on and practice God's call on our lives and our communities of faith. In my United Methodist tradition, that focus, purpose, or mission is "making disciples of Jesus Christ for the transformation of the

---

[1] Stephen R. Covey, A. Roger Merrill, and Rebecca R. Merrill. *First Things First: To Live, to Love, to Learn, to Leave a Legacy.* New York, NY: Simon & Schuster, 1994, 75.

world." For me, everything we do as leaders in the expedition and/or the church is about guiding and motivating individuals toward that end.

While for me, mission is something a congregation or expedition and its leaders prayerfully discern to bring God's desire into focus, my friend and colleague Rev. Dr. Elmer Colyer, a scholar and theologian, disagreed, saying that mission is what God does. "Mission," he declared, "is God's action to redeem humanity, and [it] begins with God's interaction and shaping of Israel."[2] In this understanding, mission is not something that we, as humans, do. It is a loving act that flows from God, allowing us to become more like Christ. This loving action of God, this mission, begins in Israel as God begins to shape and form God's people, reaches its pinnacle in and through the person and work of Jesus Christ, and continues through us today by the power of the Holy Spirit. Mission

---

[2] Elmer M. Colyer. "Who is the Missional Triune God and What is the Missio Trinitatis?" Class Lecture, *Revitalizing the Church's Mission: Participation in the Missio Trinitatis.* University of Dubuque Theological Seminary, Doctor of Ministry, Dubuque, IA. May 20, 2020.

is an utterly Trinitarian act, flowing from
the very nature of God in and through those
whom God selects to be the instruments
through which that *Missio Trinitatis* (mission
of the Trinity) moves outward to all people
and all creation. The Trinity's mission moves
forward to the eschatological, final realization
of the New Creation that Christ will usher in
when he returns in final victory.

Our conversation grew a bit more muddled
when a student in the class said, "I thought
mission was feeding and caring for people,"
and another asked, "Isn't mission sending
money to support missionaries overseas?"

Well, which is it? Which of these definitions
of mission is correct?

You have likely heard about the parable of
the blind men who encountered an elephant.
The first, whose hand landed on the trunk,
said, "This being is like a thick snake."
Another whose hand reached its ear, said, "It
seems like a kind of fan." The third, whose
hand was upon its leg, said the elephant "is
a pillar-like a tree-trunk." The blind man
who placed his hand upon its side said, "the
elephant is like a wall." Yet another felt its

tail and described it as a rope. The last felt its tusk, stating the elephant is hard, and smooth, and like a spear.[3]

All the men in this example described an elephant, but they were referring to different parts and so came to very different conclusions. All the above conclusions were observations of the same "animal" (in this case, mission), examined from different perspectives. In our class conversation on mission, Colyer was trying to get us to see the whole elephant, while the rest of us were describing parts of it. I would agree that mission is what God does to redeem humanity, and that it begins with God's interaction with Israel.[4] Mission is God's love in action, and that love incarnate began with God's desire to redeem humanity in Israel. God's interaction and care for humanity through Israel sets the stage for the coming of Christ, and that same love continues through us today, by the power of the Holy Spirit, and continues guiding us

3   E. Bruce Goldstein, ed. *Encyclopedia of Perception.* Los Angeles, CA: SAGE, 2010, 497.

4   Elmer M. Colyer. *How to Read T. F. Torrance: Understanding His Trinitarian & Scientific Theology.* Downers Grove, IL: InterVarsity Press, 2001.

toward the ultimate reality. That mission leads us to a unique vision, which is "our attempt to anticipate in the present the *telos* of *Missio Trinitatis,* that is God's intended teleological future which is soteriological, and ecclesiological, and spans and integrates our personal lives, family, congregation, community, country, world, universe."[5] By this, Colyer means that mission is God's action to redeem humanity, and vision is a God-breathed image of the future to which God is calling.

When I talk about mission and vision in the organizational sense, I am seeking to articulate and project the intention that God has for us and our communities into the future so that we can join with God in living that reality. I am, in essence, intending an Expedition Team or congregation to ask, "How is God calling this congregation, in this place, at this time, to redeem the people that God has given us?" While mission is

---

[5] Elmer M. Colyer, Professor of Systematic Theology, Stanley Professor of Wesley Studies, and Director of the United Methodist Studies Program, University of Dubuque Theological Seminary, Dubuque, IA, in discussion with the author, Jaye Johnson, November 14, 2020. For more on this view, see Colyer, How to Read T. F. Torrance.

what God does, our role as church leaders is about how God calls us to participate in that redemption of humanity with the time, talent, and resources provided. To be clear, this definition of mission is not different from Colyer's; it is the same definition from a different angle.

As R. Paul Stevens and Phil Collins wrote in their book, *The Equipping Pastor: A Systems Approach to Congregational Leadership,* "The Church's mission is God's continuing mission. It is not merely the sum of the church's activities in the dispersed, diaspora phase of its life. Nor is mission merely something the church does as a human act, either in gratitude for salvation or in guilt for not living up to its mission mandate. It is God's mission in which we participate."[6] By this, Stevens and Collins mean that while mission in its most holistic form is about God's redemption of humanity, and while it began with Israel and culminated in Jesus, it did not end; instead,

---

[6] R. Paul Stevens and Phil Collins. *The Equipping Pastor: A Systems Approach to Congregational Leadership.* Washington, DC: Alban Institute, 1993, 132.

21

it continues today. We join with God, by the power of the Holy Spirit, in the mission to redeem humanity in our context, and we do that by focusing the resources God has given us so that we are more fully participating in God's desire and the ongoing redemption of humanity. God's call to redeem humanity must find expression in our congregations' people and must be acted upon in the ministry of our local churches. As James 2:26 reminds us, "faith without works is dead."[7]

This means that when we talk about missions as helping people through the "missions committee" or by sending money to "missions," these are – at their best – local expressions of God's desire to redeem humanity but are only pointing to the larger reality of mission. Suppose mission is about God's redemption of humanity, and our mission statements and ministries are expressions of how we intend to join God in that purpose. What, then, do I mean by accountability?

---

[7] All biblical quotations are from the *New Revised Standard Version Bible*, copyright 1989, Division of Christian Education of the National Council of Churches of Christ in the United States of America.

With your Expedition Team or study group, consider these questions:

- What do you mean when you use the word "mission"?

- What does your church mean when it uses the word "mission"?

- How is this different from the concept of mission defined here?

- How might this idea of mission reshape your journey?

Accountability

I am a fan of police dramas on TV, such as Law & Order, NCIS, and Chicago PD.

It is unusual to watch one of those shows without an attorney or police officer saying something in the aftermath of a crime like "The perpetrators of this heinous act will be held accountable!" And of course, through the magic of TV, the criminals are caught, convicted, and found guilty by the end of the hour. Scenes like that often pepper the minds of people when they think about accountability. In our world, accountability has become synonymous with a punishment to ensure responsibility is taken for some adverse action or outcome: "Whose fault is this?" Yet, this is not a biblical understanding of accountability.

Accountability, from a biblical point of view, is an attitude of grace and forgiveness. It is an act of taking on someone else's burdens and allowing them to do the same for you. Romans 12:9-13 reminds us:

> *Let love be genuine; hate what is evil, hold fast to what is good; love one another with mutual affection; outdo one another in showing honor. Do not lag in zeal, be ardent in Spirit, serve the Lord. Rejoice in hope, be patient in suffering, persevere in prayer. Contribute to the needs of the saints; extend hospitality to strangers.*

Love one another with mutual affection. This does not sound much like punishment to me!

Galatians 6:1–3 pleads with us to carry the burdens of others:

My friends, if anyone is detected in a transgression, you who have received the Spirit should restore such a one in a spirit of gentleness. Take care that you yourselves are not tempted. Bear one another's burdens, and in this way, you will fulfill the law of Christ. For if those who are nothing think they are something, they deceive themselves.

What is clear from these selections of scripture, and frankly many more, is that accountability is not about punishment from a biblical perspective. While accountability may include loving correction, that correction is never harsh or unfounded. According to David Lowes-Watson, accountability is:

Watching over one another in love for the sake of their discipleship. In the early Methodist bands, this took the form of accountability to the General Rules (do no harm, do good, stay in love with God) and for the individual's spiritual growth.[8]

What Lowes-Watson is suggesting, and rightly so, is that accountability is not detrimental, nor is it retribution. Instead, it is

---

[8] David Lowes Watson. *Covenant Discipleship: Christian Formation Through Mutual Accountability*. Eugene, OR: Wipf and Stock Publishers, 1998, 44. The phrase "do no harm, do good, and stay in love with God" is a summary of Wesley's General Rules as restated by Bishop Ruben Job in his book Three Simple Rules.

love in action: Christians care for one another.

A pastor I coach, whom I will call Grace, is a kind-hearted individual. She is peaceful, compassionate, and sympathetic to her core, and she despises conflict. To prepare for the moment when controversy would surely arise, Grace guided the board in the process of establishing a behavior covenant.

In its simplest form, a behavior covenant is a document that summarizes how congregation participants desire to be treated and how they promise to treat one another. In addition to defining these expectations, a behavior covenant also sets the procedures for precisely how the group will respond when someone violates the covenant. Put differently, a behavior covenant establishes the ground rules and procedures for how the group will navigate controversy when it emerges.

I want to make it clear that conflict is not necessarily harmful. As I define it, conflict is merely the presence of two or more ideas occupying the same space. A church must have disagreement, or it is not doing anything worth being conflicted over! A lack of conflict is an enormous conundrum because apathy is an exceedingly more complicated challenge to overcome than conflict. While disagreement is not good or bad, how churches opt to manage divergence can be healthy and beneficial or unhealthy and destructive, but conflict is indispensable to vitality.

Shortly after Grace's leaders finalized the covenant, a woman on the board arrived at a meeting visibly distraught. When asked what was upsetting her, she spewed unfounded, venomous accusations, blaming her colleagues for all the difficulties, both real and perceived, of the congregation. Following her outburst, the accuser stormed out of the room, leaving the team in dumbfounded silence.

It was a sudden, unexpected stop.

In that instant, they had to choose whether to abide by the covenant or not. With their pastor's guidance, they turned to the covenant. It spelled out unambiguously how they should manage a breach, including sharing the nature of the violation in private. Pastor Grace and a member of the board went to the offenders home and shared how she had broken the covenant. In response, the board member irately threatened to resign and abandon the church.

"No! That would be the easy way out," Grace insisted. "You are going to go back to the board and confess to breaking the covenant. You are going to abide by the promise you made to God and the others."

Those of you who loathe conflict likely have a knot in your stomach reading this. If that is the case for you, imagine how hard this conversation was for Pastor Grace. To the woman's credit, and because Pastor Grace watched over her in love, she did go back to the board; she apologized for her behavior, and more significantly, she opened up, revealing her heart and the life struggles that were overwhelming her at that moment. Through tears, she said to the board, "I need you all to help me, and I need you to pray with me to help me live out my faith and be a better Christian." The meeting culminated with everyone laying hands on the woman and praying for her. Grace reported that there was not a dry eye in the group.

There can be little question that having conversations like the one Pastor Grace and the confessing board member had is challenging. And yet it is crucial for the health and wellbeing of our congregations and our congregants. Kevin Harney, in his book *Leadership from the Inside Out: Examining the Inner Life of a Healthy Church Leader,* sums it up nicely: "Along the way, we have learned that the process is hard both for those who are disciplined and for us as leaders," He continues, "it's worth the pain to see the Holy Spirit transform hearts and lives."[9]

Caring for one another, particularly when it is complicated, reflects my characterization of accountability. Pastor Grace's situation also illustrates accountability. It would have been simple for Pastor Grace and the board to overlook the woman's conduct or let her quietly leave, but the easy thing to do is seldom the right thing. This is especially true when it comes to accountability. But the reality is that we need one another.

Accountability is about helping our siblings in Christ find their way to Jesus when they cannot do so themselves and trusting that others will do the same for us. We find an

---

[9]   Kevin Harney. *Leadership from the Inside Out: Examining the Inner Life of a Healthy Church Leader.* The Leadership Network Innovation Series. Grand Rapids, MI: Zondervan, 2007, 115.

example of this in Luke 5:17–26:

> *One day, while he was teaching, Pharisees and teachers of the law were sitting nearby (they had come from every village of Galilee and Judea and from Jerusalem); and the power of the Lord was with him to heal. Just then some men came, carrying a paralyzed man on a bed. They were trying to bring him in and lay him before Jesus; but finding no way to bring him in because of the crowd, they went up on the roof and let him down with his bed through the tiles into the middle of the crowd in front of Jesus. When he saw their faith, he said, "Friend, your sins are forgiven you." Then the scribes and the Pharisees began to question, "Who is this who is speaking blasphemies? Who can forgive sins but God alone?" When Jesus perceived their questionings, he answered them, "Why do you raise such questions in your hearts? Which is easier, to say, 'Your sins are forgiven you,' or to say, 'Stand up and walk'? But so that you may know that the Son of Man has authority on earth to forgive sins" – he said to the one who was paralyzed – "I say to you, stand up and take your bed and go to your home." Immediately he stood up before them, took what he had been lying on, and went to his home, glorifying God. Amazement seized all of them, and they glorified God and were filled with awe, saying, "We have seen strange things today."*

The man on the mat could not get to Jesus on his own; he was not able. In the same way, accountability helps others grow in faith and find their way to Jesus, especially when they are struggling to do so independently. On certain days, we are the ones carrying the mat, while on other days, we require carrying. In the Wesleyan tradition, we call this sanctification, and we cannot do it on our own. We need the Holy Spirit, and we need one another.

Accountability is looking over one another in love. It is caring for the wellbeing and souls of those we are in covenant with. It is about challenging them when their behavior is contrary to what they say they wish to be and celebrating alongside them when they excel. If accountability is looking over one another in love, accountability is not about judgment, guilt, ought, or should. Accountability is about having partners to help carry the burden when you cannot.

With your Expedition Team or study group, consider these questions and tasks:

- What would happen in your church if someone yelled at the board and stormed out like the woman in Pastor Grace's church?

- Do you welcome or resist accountability individually? Why?

- What about your church and your Expedition Team? Do you collectively welcome or resist accountability?

- If you were to write a covenant together for your congregation or team, what might go into it?

- Discuss a time when you experienced accountability.

CHAPTER FOUR

The Journey of Missional Accountability

If mission is about God's redemption of humanity, and accountability is looking over one another in love, then missional accountability is looking over one another and the church in love to make sure that together we stay focused on joining God in redeeming the world. This looking over one another for the sake of the mission occurs in a dynamic way and is never static; the interplay between spiritual growth (the vehicle), leadership (the driver), and purpose (the destination) is always shifting.

As we continue our journey through understanding missional accountability, let us explore each of these components of missional accountability and how they relate to one another.

Spiritual Growth: The Vehicle of Missional Accountability

Mark was a life-long Methodist who grew up in the church. His great-grandparents were charter members of the church. His family had been worshiping in that community for 150 years. I sat down in Mark's office one day, something I did from time to time. He said, "Tell me something, Pastor, when did the rules change?" At that time, Mark, who was in his 70s, said he thought being a Christian was about trying to be a "good person," coming to church on Sunday, putting your check in the plate, and serving on a committee when asked. "But now you seem to be telling me we must focus on our faith all the time, we need to use our gifts to make a difference in the world, and we need to think about faith not just on Sunday but every day. I hear you teaching that being Christian is a 24/7 proposition," he said. "Tell me, when did the rules change?"

The rules have not changed. Our understanding of church and our expectations over the years most certainly have changed, but not for the better. The reality is that for numerous years, what Mark described was what people believed being a faithful Christian entailed. The terms "Christian" and "church member" have been conflated. Being a good church member is not necessarily what it means to be a faithful Christian; we have confused the two. As Phil Maynard says in his book *Shift 2: Helping Congregations Back into The Game of Effective Ministry,* we have settled for making members and ceased making disciples.[10] Mark was taking a Disciple Bible study class and was becoming awakened to faith in new ways. Until that point, discipleship was not on Mark's radar. Being a good, responsible church member was his focus.

Discipleship is about growing in faith to become more like Jesus. It is about loving God with all your heart, mind, soul, and strength and loving your neighbor as yourself. As Junius Dotson puts it, "Not fully understanding the why of discipleship weakens our ability to make disciples, and it ultimately weakens our witness to the world. One cannot give away something we do not have."[11] Dotson says a disciple:

---

[10] Phil Maynard. *Shift 2: Helping Congregations Come Back into the Game of Effective Ministry,* Market Square Books, 2019, Shift 3.

[11] Junius B. Dotson. *Developing an Intentional Discipleship System: A Guide for Congregations. See All The People.* Nashville, TN: Discipleship Ministries, 2017, 20.

- Worships

- Is part of a community

- Commits to spiritual practices

- Is generous and serves

- Is seeking to be Christ-like.[12]

These marks of discipleship are basically another way to reaffirm the The United Methodist membership vows, in which we promise to offer our prayers, presence, gifts, witness, and service. If you are from another faith tradition, fear not, for these vows are based on Jesus' words in Luke 10:27: "He [Jesus] answered, 'You shall love the Lord your God with all your heart, and with all your soul, and with all your strength, and with all your mind; and your neighbor as yourself.'"

Discipleship is about listening for and following God, and it is not only for the hyper-religious. As Harney writes, "Hearing and recognizing God's voice isn't just for the monastic or the zealot. It should be the normative daily experience of every Christian

---

[12] Dotson, 26.

leader. Jesus, the Good Shepherd, makes it clear that his sheep recognize his voice. This is the only way we can follow him."[13]

While I would prefer that all those who call your congregation their faith home would strive to meet these marks of discipleship, it is especially critical for those of you serving as leaders in of your congregation! As Dotson states,

> *Intentional discipleship begins when authentic leaders model what it means to be a growing, maturing disciple. Leadership at all levels must be honest and vulnerable, sharing how they are growing in their faith as they lead others, while encouraging others in their journey. We should see every team gathering as an opportunity to not only accomplish administrative or ministry tasks, but also to provide time for accountability to growing spiritually. In essence, much like the historic Methodist class system, every team would operate like a small group.*[14]

Small groups, life groups, accountability groups, class meetings – call them what you will; the desired outcome is the same: having

---

[13] Harney, 63.

[14] Dotson, 32.

others on this journey of faith with you. These groups have the power, or at least the potential, to be channels for the Holy Spirit to work to knock down barriers, bringing diverse people with radically different views of life together in Christ's name.

For four years, I gathered weekly with several area pastors. We asked one another: "How is it with your soul?" In that group, we shared intimate details of how we struggled with life and leadership. We shared deep sorrow and disappointment and celebrated together with joy how God was working in our lives and our communities of faith. We met every week with few exceptions.

I am a fast-paced leader. I am task-oriented and would rather not waste time. If you share those personality traits, you might wonder how I could give up two or three hours every week. I "gave up" that time while pastoring a growing church. We merged with another church, created a new one with a new shared vision, and eventually built a new building. The time spent in prayer and personal discipleship with my colleagues in Christ was not a waste of time in any way, shape, or form, nor was it "time away" from the church. It was fuel to help me lead to the best of my ability, often well beyond what I could do on my own.

That weekly time dedicated to prayer and sharing allowed me to see past the divisions of our world and congregation to live more fully in God's purpose. Leading a church is not easy; I believe it is one of the hardest things any group can do, especially in this hyper-partisan, hostile world. Maybe you, too, have noticed the overarching theme of division in our world today – frankly, it is hard to miss. While disagreements and diverse ways of looking at the world have always been part of our collective experience, the chasm appears to be becoming more prominent. Common ground is becoming ever more challenging to identify. One group says the box is black; the other says it is white. Neither has ever heard of the color gray, and both are sure they are correct.

Social media has fueled this growing sense of division. There is a sense of safety and freedom online that allows people with radically divergent views to express themselves in ways they would not ordinarily do face to face. If you have ever used social media, you can likely personally attest to watching what begins as respectful dialogue devolve into juvenile displays of name-calling. In response to these reactions, social media is conditioning us to seek like-minded people with whom we already agree, so we do not have to worry about harsh attacks or guarding our words. If you wish to read more about how social media impacts our society, you might check out *Too Much of a Good Thing: Are You Addicted to Your Smartphone?* by James Roberts.[15]

It is obvious that our inability to communicate across theological, political, and sociological lines in civilized ways is growing exponentially more difficult, but that trajectory need not continue. Accountability can bridge that growing abyss and draw us closer to one another to offer an alternative model of conversation for the world. One of my weekly accountability groups' most exhilarating aspects was that we were theologically and politically in very different places.

We seldom agreed on human sexuality,

---

[15] James A. Roberts. *Too Much of a Good Thing: Are You Addicted to Your Smartphone?* 2016.

politics, or issues of the day. And yet, what drew us together, what united us, was Christ. Devotion to Christ, dedication to one another, and commitment to our communities permitted us to grow personally and spiritually. Guided by the Holy Spirit, we were drawn closer to one another and Christ despite our radically different ways of looking at the world.

While being part of a small group is critical to spiritual growth, and spiritual growth is essential to healing our culture's divides, teachers and preachers need to be incredibly diligent. If you read scripture to teach or lead others, you mustn't fall victim to a common temptation to exchange lesson preparation for personal devotion. As Harney has it, "Christian leaders, particularly those in church ministry, are often tempted to substitute their lesson preparation for personal time feeding on the rich banquet of God's Word. This is problematic because our minds and hearts turn differently when we are getting ready to teach."[16]

By this, Harney rightly means that we

---

[16] Harney, 46.

must not allow church responsibilities to replace our devotional time as leaders, lay, or clergy. While preparing to teach others, we tend to look for unique facts, exciting meanings, and aspects of a particular scripture that will engage others. While reading scripture for our spiritual journey, guided by the Holy Spirit, we seek God to speak a personal and unique message to us.

What is clear is that faith cannot be a solitary journey. We need fellow travelers united in nothing more than a sincere desire to follow Christ.

"Who are your traveling companions?" asks Michael Slaughter. "Each of us is responsible for developing our networks of mentoring relationships."[17]

Frankly, this is not something that comes naturally to me. Since moving to a new community, I have yet to find another group I feel as comfortable going as deep with as I did with that group; I miss it very much.

---

[17] Michael Slaughter. *Momentum for Life: Biblical Principles for Sustaining Physical Health, Personal Integrity, and Strategic Focus.* Rev. ed. Nashville, TN: Abingdon Press, 2008, 98.

Thus far, I have made the case that the first step to missional accountability is spiritual growth and getting connected to others on the journey. When you find that sense of community, that renewed connection to Christ through others, it can be tempting to let that be the end. It is not an end, though, but the vehicle in which your congregation travels.

With your Expedition Team or study group, consider these questions:

- Who is on your spiritual journey with you?

- Who, other than your family or pastor, prays with and for you?

- Are you currently in a group like the one described? Why or why not?

- Why do you think people resist these types of relationships?

- What is one thing your Expedition Team or church can do to encourage these types of relationships in your congregation?

CHAPTER FIVE
Using Our Spiritual Gifts

I run into many church leaders, clergy, and laity who tell me they are tired. They are ready for someone else to take on the responsibilities of running the church. Some of them mean it! And yet tiredness is a symptom of over-functioning. "Being tired and being effective are far from the same thing," Claims Gil Rendle in his book *Quietly Courageous,* "Tiredness can appear noble to anxious people who are comforted knowing that someone is working tirelessly on their behalf. However, being tired is not evidence of being a good leader. Tiredness is not necessarily evidence of wisely using limited human resources for purpose rather than for comfort."[18]

---

[18] Gilbert R. Rendle. *Quietly Courageous: Leading the Church in a Changing World.* Lanham, MD: Rowman & Littlefield, 2019, 194.

Church leaders often lead in a way that seeks to soothe people and keep them pleased rather than enticing them to join God's call to redeem humanity. Refusing to take the easy way in favor of the right way is crucial. If seeking new things ceases, to keep people happy, congregations end up surrendering to the whims of people's moods. This is a problem because, as Michael Slaughter puts it,

> *God gives big visions to people who are willing to take big actions! Leadership implements the risky strategic actions necessary to reach God's place of promise. Doers are driven by visions and dreams and not by expectations or reprisals of people. They are compelled forward by truth, not motivated by the accolades of committees. Leaders do the right thing rather than the expected thing.*[19]

Doing the right thing, not the easy thing, is so challenging that leaders get weary, causing people to second-guess their decisions. Tiredness can prevent leaders from accomplishing what is challenging yet necessary. Another source of tiredness is leading out of a sense of duty rather than out of our spiritual giftedness.

---

[19] Slaughter, 101.

One example of leading out of a sense of duty – of "ought"– can be found in numerous churches' insistence on using clipboards and sign-up sheets. When a sign-up sheet is passed around to countless individuals, there is an overwhelming sense of guilt, causing people to sign up. On the one hand, this is an efficient way to get volunteers; on the other hand, it causes individuals to volunteer for ministry activities that they neither enjoy nor excel in.

At one church where I coached, it was common practice to pass around sign-up sheets to get liturgists to help lead worship. While this method efficiently recruited the necessary volunteers, many people signed up because they felt they ought to sign up; they did so out of a sense of duty and obligation, not because it was within their area of giftedness. This resulted in volunteers leading worship who were not called. These folks neither liked, nor were even particularity good at serving in that capacity. Their lack of enthusiasm for the service they volunteered for was apparent. The result would have been drastically improved had that church prayerfully recruited three or four people who felt called to lead worship out of their gifts, rather than tapping into people's sense of guilt. Those who engage in a ministry because they feel they should burn out quickly, and the lack of passion infects the congregation.

To abandon the "oughts," your Expedition Team (or study group) – and eventually, all those who join your community of faith – should seek to discover their passions, callings, and gifts and direct them toward making a difference in the world. As John Burke writes, "Spiritual gifts need to be pursued, discovered and developed. As you do this, you'll find they energize you and build up the Body to meet needs."[20] Tiredness and burnout in church leadership, both laity and clergy, occurs primarily because leaders over-function, micro-manage, and are often placed in roles that do not use their God-given spiritual gifts.

Leading out of your spiritual gifts energizes and leads to participation in God's mission, but countless church leaders do not

---

[20] John Burke. *Soul Revolution: How Imperfect People Become All God Intended.* Grand Rapids, MI: Zondervan, 2008, 209.

take the time to discover those gifts, and others are simply unaware of their gifts. I was leading a Disciple Bible study retreat to wrap up our study. The Holy Spirit had transformed lives and hearts in our 36 weeks together, so the group had become very close-knit. As part of the wrap-up retreat, I had people take a spiritual gift inventory, and everyone in the group made their personal assessment as well as an assessment of the others. In other words, people could compare what they thought their gifts were with what others saw in them.

One woman, whom I will call Shirley, looked at the gift assessment and said, "I do not have any gifts!" Before I had a chance to speak up, members of the group said, "You are kind and caring. You have the gift of hospitality, and you are always willing to do whatever needs doing." Another pointed out that she and her husband were mentoring a young couple in the church. Yet another said to Shirley, "Your deep faith is an inspiration to me. You help me be a better follower of Jesus by your example."

Shirley started weeping tears of joy and gratitude. She did not know her spiritual gifts, but that did not mean she did not have or use them. It took a community to help her identify her gifts. From that point onward, Shirley thrived in ministry, using her gifts with a newfound enthusiasm.

With your Expedition Team or study group, consider these questions and tasks:

- What are you doing in the church or expedition that drains you?

- What are you doing in the church or expedition that gives life?

- Why does one drain and the other energize?

- Discuss these with your fellow travelers on your Expedition Team or church and develop a plan for ways to spend more time doing the things that energize you.

CHAPTER SIX

Leadership: The Driver of Missional Accountability

Thus far, I have defined mission as joining God in God's desire to redeem humanity, accountability as watching over one another in love, spiritual growth as becoming more Christ-like, and intimated spiritual growth as the vehicle for missional accountability. While spiritual growth is this vehicle and contains all that we need for our journey with Jesus, a vehicle is useless without a driver. Leadership is that driver.

Leadership is about directing the congregation's resources, energy, and passion into the world. It is about how we inspire people to live boldly in God's preferred future. In the United Methodist Church, the Pastor is the chair of the nominations committee. The intention of that committee is to discover and develop lay leadership. As chair of that committee over the years, I have made desperate phone calls begging people to take this position or that whenever there were spots to fill on committees and time is of the essence. As the charge conference (annual meeting) approached each fall, "I will take a name, any name" became the unofficial mantra when it was time to find new leaders. Perhaps you have made or received similar calls, but frantically calling everyone because you require a name to complete a form is not leadership – not exceptional leadership, in any case.

While I intuitively knew that selecting leaders in this haphazard manner was not an exceptional way to lead, I was driven by practicality. But that all changed after making one of those random calls. I contacted a woman from our congregation and asked her to be on a committee. Her response changed how I thought about leadership development. She said, "Pastor, I could do that job, and I could do it well. However, I do not sense that God is calling me to it, so If I said 'yes,' I would be taking that opportunity from someone who is." I was so stunned by the beauty of that statement that it took me a moment to realize she said "no," even if it was the best "no" I had ever heard.

That conversation transformed the way I asked people to be in leadership positions. It made me realize that leadership is fundamentally about helping people find their passion and directing that passion toward making a difference in the world to facilitate God's preferred future.[21]

Stephen Covey encapsulates this sentiment when he writes, "Simply put – at its most elemental practical level – leadership is communicating to people their worth and potential so clearly that they come to see it in themselves."[22] This means that leadership is not so much about making decisions, being in charge, or doing the work yourself as it is about discovering and unleashing others' potential. It is about finding your voice, and once you do, helping others find theirs. Helping people find their voice is the place where conscience, passion, talent, and

---

[21] Stephen R. Covey. *The 8th Habit: From Effectiveness to Greatness.* New York, NY: Free Press, 2004, 74.

[22] Covey, 8th Habit, 98.

need overlap.[23] This is a fundamental aspect of leadership and is necessary to steer the vehicle, but it is only part of the equation; leaders also need to think about helping the organization find its voice.

As Michael Jacoby Brown writes in his book *Building Powerful Community Organizations: A Personal Guide to Creating Groups That Can Solve Problems and Change the World*:

> *Leaders think about and develop the leadership of other people in the organization. They ask: What does this person need in order to develop his or her leadership? What is his or her next step in taking responsibility for the organization? Leaders also think about the whole group and what it needs. What does the group as a whole need to be stronger? How can a group find its power and voice?*[24]

Leaders guide individuals and the organization toward the subsequent step on the road to a broader vision. While secular

---

[23] Covey, 8th Habit, 5.

[24] Michael Jacoby Brown. *Building Powerful Community Organizations: A Personal Guide to Creating Groups That Can Solve Problems and Change the World.* Arlington, MA: Long Haul Press, 2006, 188.

leaders steer individuals and organizations toward the next step, Christian leaders must additionally contemplate God's calling on the organization to determine what that subsequent step will be and how it will be faithful. Christian leaders are stewards of the resources entrusted to their care that enables God's vision to become a reality. As Stevens and Collins assert, "Christian leadership is the God-given ability to influence others so that believers will trust and respond to the Head of the church for themselves, in order to accomplish the Lord's purposes for God's people in the world."[25] To support people and the organization in joining God, leaders need to focus on what is occurring inside and outside the congregation.

While in motion, a driver of an actual automobile needs to be attentive to what is happening inside and outside the car. Inside the car, a driver must pay attention to gages, other passengers, the ever-critical music selection, and more. At the same time, an operator must also notice what is transpiring

---

[25] Stevens and Collins, 109.

outside the car, such as other vehicles, the weather, road hazards, and traffic signs. In the same way, leadership has two areas of focus: discovering and unleashing others' gifts and talents, and shepherding the whole organization in taking the next faithful step. Finding and using the gifts of individuals is akin to what is happening inside the car, while steering the organization is analogous to a driver focusing on what is happening in the environment outside the vehicle.

Paying attention to what is happening both inside and outside the congregation is essential. Without being crystal clear on the critical next steps for the congregation, it is impossible to direct the use of God-given gifts in beneficial ways. Even if you have people willing to use their talents, lack of clarity on the exact next steps leads to energy without power. It causes confusion and chaos. Conversely, if leaders know the next faithful step but cannot harness and develop passions and talents to act, we end up with a pipe dream that does not reflect reality.

If drivers must focus on activity inside and outside the congregation, where should leaders begin? Leaders should begin by interrupting familiar patterns of behavior to create space for others to step up. Brown makes the case that leaders need to continually ask if they are sucking up so much responsibility that they provide no room for others to take it? Are they "practicing the 'iron rule' of organizing – never do for people what they can do for themselves?"[26] Church leaders often over-function, and this denies developing leaders the opportunity to lead.

A man named Stan served a church that grew larger than ever during his tenure. I was his coach, and one of my persistent questions was, "What are you doing that someone else can do?" This question was not comfortable for him to answer because he sensed an obligation to be in charge. For him, being in charge meant completing the bulk of the work himself because he was the compensated professional. In other words, he thought that was the job. He did not know any other way. Not only did Stan do everything himself, but he also thought it was his role as Pastor. He

---

[26] M. J. Brown, 209.

also got a psychological ego boost from the church's growth, but he soon realized that the model was unsustainable.

Stan came to recognize that his model of leadership could not last, and he did something difficult: He moved from being the primary doer of the ministry to being the primary enabler/equipper of the ministry. The congregation bloomed because Stan gave up control of all things to focus on the few things that only he could manage. He concentrated on letting go of all but three things: mission and vision, preaching and worship, and developing leaders. While pastors of growing churches do not do these three things entirely independently, they must be the principal driver in these areas if a congregation is to thrive.

Stan's pre-growth leadership style is emblematic of countless church leaders, both laity and clergy. Church leaders over-function. In the Midwest, where I live, there is a formidable work ethic deeply rooted in agricultural backgrounds. This work ethic tends to propel individuals for generations after leaving the farm.

My grandfather was a farmer, and my dad grew up on the farm. Our unofficial family motto growing up was, "You cannot control how smart you are. You can control how hard you work." Therefore, the absolute worst insult you could heave upon someone was to call them "lazy." While this strong work ethic serves me well in many ways, it also drives me to overwork and over-function. Like Stan, in the past, I have operated from a misguided notion that as the professional, it is my responsibility to personally do all the work I possibly could, only delegating what is beyond that. That is a flawed leadership style.

There is a fundamental flaw in a leader-does-it-all approach, as David Marquet, a former Navy submarine commander, points out in his book *Turn the Ship Around! A True Story of Turning Followers into Leaders*:

> *Delegation is the exception, not the rule [...]*
> *While that singular point of accountability is*
> *attractive in many ways, there is a downside [...]*
> *There is no incentive or reward for developing*
> *mechanisms that enable excellence beyond your*
> *immediate tour.*[27]

---

[27] L. David Marquet. *Turn the Ship Around! A True Story of Turning Followers into Leaders.* New York, NY: Portfolio, 2012, 41.

Navy commanders were promoted or not based on how smoothly and efficiently things operated when they were in command. They were not responsible for anything before they arrived or the moment after they departed.

The Navy's leadership model was understandably built on the idea of one primary leader, the commanding officer, and the rest of the crew were, to lesser or greater degrees, followers. This leadership model is attractive because it is clear who is in charge, who has the responsibility, and who is ultimately at fault if something goes wrong. However, this command structure fails to consider the systemic issues that contribute to success or failure. This model of leadership is often called solo-heroic leadership.[28]

In the church, solo-heroic leadership implies that the right clergy leader can make everything perfect and fix all the problems a congregation may face. If anyone was capable of what is called "solo-heroic leadership," it was Jesus – the Son of God. And yet, Jesus did

---

[28] A term introduced to me by Greg Survant and Christin Nevins of Spiritual Leadership, Inc. https://www.spiritual-leadership.org/

not lead that way. Instead, he called others, assisted in discovering their gifts, gave them all they needed, and sent them out to use those gifts in his name:

> *All authority in heaven and on earth has been given to me. Go therefore and make disciples of all nations, baptizing them in the name of the Father and of the Son and of the Holy Spirit, and teaching them to obey everything that I have commanded you. And remember, I am with you always, to the end of the age.*[29]

Like the Navy, churches have systems that reward leaders for what materializes when they are "in charge" and not for what occurs when they pass the mantle. The difficulty, as Steve Chalke points out in his book *Change Agents: 25 Hard-Learned Lessons in the Art of Getting Things Done,* is that "great leadership is measured by what's left after you're gone."[30] Effective leadership, especially in the church, is not about doing the work alone. It is about training and developing others so that the

---

[29] Mathew 28:18–20.

[30] Steve Chalke. *Change Agents: 25 Hard-Learned Lessons in the Art of Getting Things Done.* Grand Rapids, MI: Zondervan, 2007, 61.

ministry continues when the originators move on. Otherwise, when they seek new challenges, the excellent ministry that has been initiated unravels, leaving the church and the ministry in shambles.

With your Expedition Team or study group, consider these questions:

- Who is the best leader inside or outside the church you can name?

- What makes that person a great leader? What do they do differently than other people?

- Think about the people on *The Greatest Expedition* journey with you. Who are the leaders on your team? Why did you name them?

- What does it mean to be a Christian leader?

- What does it mean to be a leader in your church?

- Do you consider yourself a leader in your congregation? Why or why not?

CHAPTER SEVEN

Leadership vs. Managment

Leadership, which is the driver of missional accountability, is about helping individuals discover their gifts and enabling them to use those gifts to move the congregation toward God's preferred future. There is, however, a second subset of leadership that we need to name: management.

Leadership and management may appear to be equivalents. While both are critical to the health of an organization, they must not be conflated. Leadership tells us which way we are heading; management tells us the best and most efficient way to get there. Visionary leadership without management stalls with little progress, while management without leadership tends to very efficiently accomplish things of little importance.

As Lovett Weems claims, "Leaders do not manage or administrate, manipulate, or dictate, process or enable, – they lead."[31] Leadership always points people and organizations toward the next faithful step in creating something more significant than the sum of the parts. In their book *Leadership on the Line: Staying Alive through the Dangers of Leading,* Ronald Heifetz and Martin Linsky argue that leadership is worth the risk because goals extend beyond material gain or personal advancement by making the lives of people around you better. Leadership provides meaning and creates purpose. The pair state, "We believe that every human being has something unique to offer, and that a larger sense of purpose comes from using that gift to help your organization, families, or communities thrive."[32]

Leadership drives the vehicle. Leadership keeps the church or expedition on track,

---

[31] Lovett H. Weems. *Church Leadership: Vision, Team, Culture, and Integrity.* Nashville, TN: Abingdon Press, 1993, 27.

[32] Ronald A. Heifetz and Martin Linsky. *Leadership on the Line: Staying Alive through the Dangers of Leading.* Boston, MA: Harvard Business School Press, 2002, 3.

makes steering corrections, and pays attention to what is happening outside and inside the vehicle. Leaders are visionary people, as E. Carver McGriff and M. Kent Millard call them, and they:

- Take time for quiet thoughtfulness

- Spend time with people

- Stay in touch with the real world

- Read

- Refuse to get bogged down in the minutiae of the everyday activities

- Spend time with leaders of the congregation.[33]

Paraphrasing Covey, I would add that leaders stay focused on what matters most – the purpose of why we exist. Purpose is the destination of missional accountability.

---

[33] E. Carver McGriff and M. Kent Millard. *The Passion Driven Congregation.* Nashville, TN: Abingdon Press, 2003, 44-46.

With your Expedition Team or study group, consider these questions:

- How does your church and Expedition Team decide what is most important?

- What drives decision-making in your church or expedition? (E.g., the way you have always done it, the mission, the preferences of the leadership, the Pastor, the desires and wishes of a small group, or something else?)

- How do you discern what God is calling you to do?

CHAPTER EIGHT

Purpose: The Destination of Missional Accountability

If spiritual growth is the vehicle and leadership is the driver, we still need a destination. Purpose is the destination of missional accountability. Purpose is that which reveals, defines, and shapes the future. The purpose must inspire people to live courageously in God's preferred future. Knowing the destination of your congregation is critical if you hope to invite others to join the journey.

While it is challenging to recruit people to join a congregation's journey if they cannot grasp the destination, it is also critical that the congregation aligns to assure movement in a unified direction. As Brown explains, "Effective groups require clear boundaries, including a common perspective on core issues. Openness to other perspectives may seem nice, but in actuality this approach can destroy the group before it is launched."[34] That force that keeps the group together and moving in the same direction is vision. "Vision is seeing with the mind's eye what is possible in people, in projects, causes, and enterprises. Vision results when our mind joins need with possibility."[35] Purpose is about direction. It is the filter through which all a church does must pass. Purpose creates excitement, brings people together, and motivates them toward a shared reality.

Shared reality and common purpose draw people together when they can appreciate the reasoning behind a congregation's ministry. Ken Willard clarifies, "Many mission statements in business and church organizations will contain some element of purpose."[36] While reflecting on the United Methodist statement of the mission "to make disciples of Jesus Christ for the

---

[34] M. J. Brown, 63.

[35] Covey, 8th Habit, 65.

[36] Ken Willard. *Greatest Expedition Resource on Mission, Vision, and Core Values,* Market Square Books, 2021.

transformation of the world," Willard suggests transforming the world is the purpose because it "explains 'why' we are doing the 'what.'" Nothing can rejuvenate a disheartened congregation faster than remembering its purpose.[37] As Rick Warren says in the now-somewhat-dated (but still helpful) *Purpose Driven Church,* "A clear purpose defines what we do, and it defines what we don't do."[38]

My wife – you know, the one who has an entirely different travel style to mine – is much smarter than me. She often says, "The death of any ministry is to name it the first annual so and so." Why? Because the name suggests that the ministry will continue in perpetuity. It makes it so that we engage in annual ministry long after forgetting the need for that ministry or after that need no longer exists. It is clarity of purpose that allows us to know what things, even beloved things, we need to let go of to pick up the very best.

---

[37] Richard Warren. *The Purpose Driven Church: Growth without Compromising Your Message & Mission.* Grand Rapids, MI: Zondervan, 1995, 82.

[38] Warren, 87.

Warren continues, "If you want to build a healthy, strong, and growing church, you must spend time laying a solid foundation. This is done by clarifying in the minds of everyone involved exactly why the church exists and what it is supposed to do."[39]

One might think that getting clear about the purpose of a congregation or expedition could be difficult, but I doubt you think it would be painful. And yet, a peculiar phenomenon occurs when purpose is clarified and a church says, "This is who we are." It is impossible to announce this without at the same time saying, "This is who we are not." A congregation clear about who it is not must say "no" to ideas for ministry that are inconsistent with that purpose.

Saying "no" is exceedingly difficult when your prayerfully discerned purpose does not support a beloved ministry, but it is a critical aspect of missional accountability. I spent months working with a church leadership team to determine who God was inviting them to be. After the purpose was clarified

---

[39] Warren, 86.

and the leaders were able to reimagine a new future, enthusiasm peaked. The leadership made different decisions and tried new things that were consistent with the vision they were discerning; some failed, but most were a fantastic success.

One member of the leadership team, Debbie, was a life-long member of the church and a long-time organizer of the church's much-loved annual fall bazaar and bake sale. This event had been part of this church's history for more than 50 years, and Debbie had been the champion of that ministry for 25 years. Debbie arrived at one meeting visibly troubled. In the spiritual formation portion of the meeting, someone asked if she was okay.

"No. I am not okay. I am distraught," Debbie said. "I believe with all my heart that God is calling us to live into this vision as a church."

Another team member said, "I am sorry you are troubled, but why does that upset you?"

Debbie replied, "Because I do not see how the bazaar fits that vision and in good conscience, I cannot continue to organize it, nor do I think we should do it anymore because it is not consistent with who God is calling us to be in this time and place."

The room was dead silent. Again, one of those sudden stops.

The leadership team decided that night to end the beloved fall bazaar because it no longer fit the church's vision. The team decided to cease a treasured ministry, with half a century of history, knowing full well that it would cause great angst within the congregation. Still, they felt it was a necessary in keeping with the new vision.

In steering the congregation toward its destination, they made a course correction. In place of the bazaar, the church adopted a neighborhood elementary school. Members read to kids, bought supplies, supported teachers, and volunteered for the school mentoring program, letting the prayer team know when they would be mentoring a student so that the team could pray at that time for that mentor and mentee. Just to be clear, for confidentiality reasons, the kids' names were not shared with the church. The church set up a discretionary fund and gave access to the principal, saying, "You know what our kids need; use these funds to meet those needs, and let us know when you need more."[40] The principal regularly updated the leadership, sharing stories of how the church's ministry was impacting lives. Eventually, he was so impressed by the church's work and witness that he joined, as did many teachers and families from that school.

Had the bazaar continued as it always had, or if Debbie had refused to offer its ending for consideration, the church would have lacked the energy to enter into that bold partnership with the school. Two years later, the church brought back the bazaar, working in partnership with the school. This time, rather than using it as a fundraiser for the church, all the money they made was donated to the school and the faculty, staff, and parents helped staff the event.

Debbie experienced discomfort caused by the clarifying of the church's purpose and vision. She realized that the church's proposed destination could not include something she cared about, but to her credit, she followed

---

[40] This idea is not original to this congregation.

God's purpose and not her preference. This clarity of vision allowed Debbie to tolerate the pain of letting go of the bazaar. As Janet Cawley observed in her book *Who is Our Church: Imagining Congregational Identity:*

> *The truth will make you free, but first it will make you miserable. Sometimes the truth is painful...but if there was some promise that pain was going to lead somewhere – to freedom or healing or reconciliation – you could face it. But without that premise?"* [41]

In other words, without the promise of what the future could hold and a picture of what could be possible, it would have been inconceivable for Debbie and the rest of the congregation to even contemplate letting go of a ministry as cherished as the bazaar.

Purpose and vision show us the path to the destination. Weems rightly points out that vision defines the purpose of a congregation, maps a direction, and inspires congregants to take the next faithful step. Weems writes, "The function of vision is to unite, energize,

---

[41] Janet R. Cawley. *Who Is Our Church? Imagining Congregational Identity.* Herndon, VA: Alban Institute, 2006, 35–36.

focus, becomes the standard, raises sights, draws and invites others."[42] While making the destination clear unifies, there are also pitfalls. Clear vision must always lead to dissatisfaction with what currently exists, as it did for Debbie. Clear purpose exposes a gap between what is and what is desired, but closing that gap is impossible without a destination.

If you do not have a destination in mind while traveling, you do not know where to turn or in which direction to go. There may be disagreement in the car. Without a clear vision, that critical space fills with the wants, desires, and demands of people who have the power to force their will on the congregation or the expedition. "If a compelling vision is not present, or if the organization is not seeking a vision, then a vacuum is created," writes Weems. "The result will be either no vision or, more likely, the presence of many small competing visions. In either case, the result is decline."[43]

---

[42] Weems, 66–67.

[43] Weems, 29.

If you are planning a trip but do not know where you are going, it is tough to prepare, and it is impossible to navigate a vehicle toward that destination. Therefore, churches and Expedition Teams need to be clear that spiritual growth is the vehicle, leadership is the driver that keeps the car on the road and the correct route, and purpose is the destination. Although these are the three keys thus far, we know that driving is more complicated and requires awareness of our surroundings.

Missional Accountability (the journey)

SPIRITUAL GROWTH
THE VEHICLE

PURPOSE
THE DESTINATION

LEADERSHIP
THE DRIVER

CHAPTER EIGHT
It Takes All Three

When I was in college, some good friends were trying to drive from Des Moines, Iowa, to Storm Lake, Iowa. Storm Lake, home of Buena Vista University, is two and a half hours northwest of Des Moines. My friends started driving and were enjoying the journey. About an hour and a half later, my friends were making excellent time – until they crossed the border into Missouri.

They were going the wrong way!

My friends needed a GPS system to guide them. They needed to pay attention to the direction of travel, the signs, and the landmarks. Missional accountability does that for congregations. It prevents going to Missouri when our destination is in Iowa.

While there are many things you might

like to have for a road trip, it is impossible to drive anywhere without a destination, a vehicle, and a driver. It takes all three of these elements working together for a successful road trip. What might happen to road trip plans if any one of these three were missing? A driver and a vehicle but no destination would lead to driving around aimlessly. On the other hand, a destination and a vehicle but no driver would lead to going nowhere fast. Finally, a destination and a driver but no vehicle would lead to walking, making for a pretty miserable road trip!

When it comes to missional accountability, as with road trips, all three elements are essential: spiritual growth (the vehicle), leadership (the driver), and the destination (the purpose). If any of these three is missing or not operating on all cylinders, missional accountability stalls, and the journey stops.

To be clear, all congregations and expeditions have these three components. However, successful churches have the right vehicle, driver, and destination. They are also always fine-tuning, clarifying, and improving those components, striving to be

Christ-centered and focused on partnering
with God to make a difference in their context.

Some congregations are struggling,
trying to travel in the wrong vehicle. My
wife and I own several vehicles. We have a
tiny subcompact car that gets fantastic gas
mileage. We also own an enormous, one-ton
diesel pickup. These two vehicles have some
things in common. They each have four
wheels, a steering wheel, an engine, etc. But
they have very different uses that are not
interchangeable. If we want to pull our camper,
we do not take our little car. Similarly, if we
are taking a long trip with just the two of us,
we will take our small car to save gas – plus,
our F-350 is a bit of a tank, and it rides like
one. For long trips without the camper, the car
is clearly the better choice. While spiritual
growth is the appropriate vehicle for missional
accountability, churches use various vehicles
to carry their congregations.

I was a guest preacher at a church with
two worship services. In between services,
I sat in with an adult Sunday school class
as they discussed immigration. I listened
to the debate about immigration, but what

struck me as strange was that they were not speaking about how their faith impacted their views on immigration. Instead, they were discussing how their political views informed their understandings of immigration. I asked the question, "How does your faith impact your views on this topic?" After a few moments of awkward silence, they went back to a political discussion. Later, I discovered that most of the church was not being carried forward by spiritual growth; politics was that church's vehicle.

While some churches may be trying to pull their camper with a subcompact, other congregations have the wrong driver. Amy and I have two kids. One is already in college, and the other soon will be. They are responsible, passionate, intelligent, and good-hearted people. They are also good drivers. My kids, especially my son Andrew, often corrects my bad driving habits. I am confident in their ability to drive, especially when operating their own cars. That said, I am not likely to have either of them pull our camper or drive on snowy roads. What I mean to illustrate here that just because you have a driver does not mean you have the right driver for the circumstances. Likewise, every church or expedition has leadership, but it may not be the right leadership.

One church I am acquainted with is a perfect example of what can happen when the right leaders are not at the congregation's wheel. This church is located near a busy railroad, with four trains passing feet from the church building every hour, and it did not have air conditioning. The worship team had to plan to sing a hymn every fifteen minutes because when the windows were open, no one could hear a word because a train was rattling past. The church was given a fairly large sum of money, and it made sense to add air conditioning to the building to allow the windows to be closed. The trustees and board voted "yes" to installing air conditioning and even approved a bid. But if you go to that church today, you will find faithful, delightful folks, but no air conditioning. What happened? One key leader, a parent figure for the church, said that they did not need air conditioning, ending the conversation. She imposed her view on the rest of the church. Even though official leaders had made one decision, the actual leader made a different one. This demonstrates that not all churches have the right drivers steering the congregation.

But remember, even if a church has the right driver and the proper vehicle, it cannot thrive without a particular and specific destination.

With your Expedition Team or study group, consider these questions:

- What carries your congregation forward? What carries your expedition forward? (What is the vehicle?)

- Who or what is guiding the church? Expedition? (Who or what is the driver?)

- Where is the church going? Where is the Expedition Team heading? (What is the destination?)

Spiritual Growth (the Vehicle) Is Not Enough

Growing spiritually is about loving God with all your heart, mind, soul, and strength and loving your neighbor as yourself. Doing so is the *telos*, the goal of the Christian life, but as odd as it may sound, individual spiritual growth does not lead to congregational vitality. Using extensive research, J. Russell Crabtree makes the case in Owl Sight: Evidence Base Discernment and the Promise of Organizational Intelligence for Ministry that there are three metrics to measure congregational health: energy, satisfaction, and adaptability.[44] My colleague Rev. Ryan Christenson calls this the "trifecta of congregational health."

Energy, Crabtree writes, is "a compelling purpose of message combined with a high level of engagement, in contrast, to simply watching others or going through the motions of religious activity."[45] Churches that score high in energy have a clear sense of purpose

---

[44] J. Russell Crabtree. *Owl Sight: Evidence-Based Discernment and the Promise of Organizational Intelligence for Ministry.* 2012

[45] Crabtree, 209.

and are compelled to move in that direction.

While energy measures the clarity of purpose, satisfaction gauges how content people are with the church's entire ministry. This indicator reveals where a congregation believes attention is required. Like the concept of "shalom," satisfaction is defined as "an expansive term that includes completeness, wholeness, health, peace, welfare, safety, soundness, tranquility, prosperity, perfectness, fullness, rest, harmony and the absence of agitation or discord."[46]

While energy and satisfaction reveal a vivid picture of a church's present reality, adaptability reveals how willing a congregation is to implement changes. Without an adequate adaptability level, it is much harder for leaders to steer a congregation toward the proper destination.

In his extensive research on congregations, Crabtree found that personal spiritual practices, and individual church members' growth do not correlate to marked increases

---

[46] Crabtree, 211.

in energy and satisfaction.[47] One would expect that as members' spiritual vitality increases, their church's positive energy level would also increase, but this is not the case. What Crabtree discovered is nearly a random pattern. Some churches where members bear witness to lower individual spiritual vitality levels have higher energy and satisfaction levels, and vice versa. "In fact, individual spiritual vitality contributes to only about four percent of a congregation's energy level."[48]

Assuming Crabtree is correct (and I suspect he is), while personal spiritual growth is the vehicle for congregational vitality, more is needed to make that vehicle move. Vitality depends on how spiritual growth interacts with leadership and purpose. Congregations that focus only on their members' individual spiritual growth end up with people who are too inwardly focused. They tend to see the church's purpose and faith in general as personal and private, something between them and God. However, as John Wesley

---

[47]   Crabtree, 65.

[48]   Crabtree, 40–41.

wrote, "The gospel of Christ knows of no religion, but social, no holiness but social holiness. Faith working by love is the length and breadth and depth and height of Christian perfection."[49] Wesley clearly understood that individual faith development must always result in an outward expression of that faith, and vice versa.

While spiritual growth, as I have argued, is the vehicle in which vitality must travel, that vehicle in and of itself does not lead toward vitality. A vehicle needs the right driver: It needs leadership.

Leadership (the Driver) Is Not Enough

Churches that concentrate on leadership without a clear connection to purpose also miss the mark. From the outside, these churches may seem efficient and effective. Their annual fall dinners may be spectacular, and their churches might be full; finances may not be an issue, and the people who attend may be content. Yet, a closer look likely shows a shallow spirituality and an unclear picture of

---

[49] John Wesley. *Hymns and Sacred Poems.* 1739, preface, viii.

what makes the church unique.

In stressful situations, one person or the same small group decides or relies on polity and *Robert's Rules of Order.* In some cases, the decision-makers are not in "official" leadership positions but are backseat drivers.

In smaller churches, with congregations with under 50 people in worship, the pastor and official leadership serve as advisors to the actual deciders. Larger churches that fall into this category tend to rely on denominational polity (or their interpretation of it) and *Robert's Rules of Order* when there is disagreement.

When groups get to be a specific size, rules and regulations are critical for keeping order and preventing a descent into chaos. However, in smaller groups like church boards and committees, they are unnecessary distractions and can be harmful.

Spiritually grounded leaders are able, and often even prefer, to make decisions by missional consensus. Missional consensus is agreement that God is calling the group to take a step toward God's desire. It is critical that churches who use this model do not get caught up in debating and deciding details. Once a ministry or idea is approved, and determined to be consistent with the mission, leaders need to let those who will "do" the ministry make those decisions without being micromanaged. Micromanaging details dilutes the power of this decision-making model and kills all forward momentum. Said another way, in healthy churches with the right vehicle and the proper driver, the group is always unanimous in its votes; otherwise, they do not move forward.

In this process, one person can block the group's decision if they feel it is necessary. Giving each member of the board veto power may seem cumbersome and counterproductive, but in practice, it is not, because it forces the majority to take the minority viewpoint seriously. It forces those in the minority to clearly explain and discuss their concerns and propose alternatives rather than registering their "no" vote and holding a grudge when they lose. This model promotes dialogue, partnership, and spiritual leadership, allowing the group to discern God's will.

How big of a group is too big to operate this way? I often jokingly say, "Jesus only had 12 disciples. What makes you think your team should have more?" A study of group dynamics tells us that something changes when you have over a dozen people in a room. You move from small-group dynamics, which focus on one group, to medium-group dynamics. The more people we add, the more difficult it becomes to focus on the whole group. In medium-group dynamics, we no longer have one group; we have two, three, or more smaller subsets. In other words, in a problematic discussion, we can end up with "sides," as those who are naturally more silent and reflective allow those who are more assertive and outgoing to dominate the conversation. In other words, the larger a group becomes, the more, smaller groups exist within the whole, leading to divided loyalties.[50]

Sometimes, God speaks through one person who offers what at first seems to be a very unpopular opinion. At one church I worked

[50] For an overview of group dynamics and some primary sources, see this article at https://2012books.lardbucket.org/books/sociology-brief-edition-v1.0/s07-02-group-dynamics-and-behavior.html

with, the church council was discussing financial stewardship. The church had been inviting and encouraging people to move toward tithing. To set a good example, the leaders decided to give 10% of every received weekly offering to the community. Giving away part of their weekly offering went along fine for several months until the church hit a bump in its finances. Unsurprisingly, some members of the council wanted to stop giving 10% of the weekly offering.

After much discussion, one of the leaders, whom I will call Rob, asked a straightforward yet powerful question: "What makes this conversation different from what any service organization might have in the same situation? We are talking about a lack of money and bills that need to get paid, but I have not heard one mention of how our belief in God should impact this decision."

Again, one of those sudden stops!

After a moment or two, others in the group said, "Well, of course we believe in God, but belief will not pay our bills," and returned to a vote to stop the 10 percent community tithe.

Rob grew exceedingly frustrated, stood

up, and said, "We might as well put a Lions Club logo on the front of the building and stop pretending to be a church." He stood up and walked out.[51]

After the fact, Rob felt horrible for what he saw as losing his temper, but something interesting happened when he did. The council started to rethink its decision, maintained the tithe, and shared the financial situation with the congregation the following Sunday. The offering that day was more than four times its average amount, resolving their financial struggles, and they continued to offer 10% of the weekly offering to the community. God provided.

Rob was experiencing a leadership struggle – a battle if you will – over which driver would sit at the congregation's vehicle controls and which vehicle would carry the church forward. Fear of closing, of upsetting people, and of not paying the bills, and a desire to keep things the same are all vehicles that carry some congregations.

---

[51] The Lions do wonderful work for the communities they serve. The point here is that the Lions, as a secular service organization, do not ask what God desires when making decisions. The church, on the other hand, must.

They are just not the vehicle necessary for missional accountability to thrive in a way that leads to health and vitality. The vehicle (spiritual growth) must carry the church forward because the church's leadership (the driver) must become more like Jesus to lead the church in a God-centered way.

When working with a church to select appropriate leaders, I have come to ask as many people as possible a critical question: "If you were in a spiritual crisis and your pastor was not available, who in the church would you call?" Something interesting happens when people start collecting the answers to that question. The same names start bubbling to the surface. The majority of people selected are not currently involved in the church's official leadership because they do not find it spiritually rewarding. For a church or expedition to be vital and healthy, it must practice missional accountability grounded in spirituality. The types of spiritual leaders that vital congregations need at their board table are people who are spiritually grounded and who, like Rob, will ask hard questions and refuse to make decisions as a secular organization. These leaders refuse to let God take a back seat in their decision-making.

But if a congregation is traveling in the vehicle of individual spiritual growth and has the right driver, it is still not enough: We are still missing a destination.

Purpose (the Destination) Is not Enough

I cannot count the number of times I have noticed mission and vision statements painted on walls, boldly proclaimed on bulletins and newsletters, or posted all over websites. Having a mission statement printed and posted is not awful, but it will do no good to write the purpose on walls if the ideas they reflect are not in people's hearts. The purpose must be rooted in the spiritual life of a congregation's leaders and directed toward the community.

It is not my intent to go deep into the difference between mission and vision. Ken Willard will be covering this in your next Greatest Expedition ministry tool. For my purposes, it is enough to say the mission is set in stone, does not change often, and clarifies the big picture. Vision is what God is calling us to do as we strive to live in the mission in this time and place. The vision changes over time. Other people change those two terms around, so you must carefully read mission and vision material. But no matter what you call them, both concepts are needed to paint a clear, compelling, and concise picture of the destination to which God is calling congregation.

Churches that focus on the purpose (the destination) as separate from spiritual growth (the vehicle) and leadership (the driver) end up talking a terrific game but lacking follow-through. They visualize a new reality but struggle to execute processes and programs that give birth to the vision. Churches with leaders (drivers) who are not spiritually grounded end up with a purpose (destination) that is not transformational or inspirational. Others will not be stirred to join the journey.

When helping churches understand the connection between purpose and action, I ask them, "When you drove here today, how many of you thought about the rules of the road?

Did you think about how many feet before turning you are supposed to signal? Did you think about who goes first at a stop sign? Did you have to think about when it was okay to pass and when it was not?"

Of course, most of the time, the answer to these questions is "no." I then ask them to think about what it was like when they were first learning to drive. Then, for many people, the answers to these questions are often "Yes – when I was first learning – those details were running through my head all the time." You see, writing the purpose down is only the beginning. Like a driver's manual, it shapes what we think about and how we go about driving until we can live the purpose without thinking about it.

An exact destination teaches people how to drive and how to get where you are going, whether this journey is real or metaphorical. In other words, have we, as the church, learned and taught good driving habits that reflect what is critical to this congregation/ expedition or not?

With your Expedition Team or study group, consider these questions:

- How exact is your congregation's destination? Your expedition's destination?

- How do you know it is the right destination?

- When was the last time your entire congregation or Expedition Team evaluated the destination?

- What has prevented you from moving more boldly toward your stated destination?

CHAPTER NINE

Bringing our Journey to a Close

Whether you are reading this book in your venture with *The Greatest Expedition* or reading it in your own, I hope you are developing a clear sense of what is needed to practice missional accountability to the best of your ability. My deep desire is that this resource will give you a starting place to assess your congregation and/or your expedition. I hope that it will give you the language to determine whether you have the right vehicle (spiritual growth), driver (leadership), and destination (purpose), and that you will then make plans to take steps to improve in these areas.

This type of congregational self-assessment is not easy. The more familiar we are with a congregation or expedition, the harder it is to be objective. When traveling, it often improves the experience to have a tour guide, someone who knows the area, to point out the things you might otherwise miss. This is why you have your Expedition Guide to guide your Expedition Caravan. Taking this step to engage in *The Greatest Expedition* is a great start, be sure to lean on your Expedition Guide as needed to provide those outside eyes during your expedition.

I welcome comments and questions at jayejohnsontge@gmail.com.

May God continue to bless you on *The Greatest Expedition*!

Selected Bibliography and Works Cited

Beaumont, Susan. *How to Lead When You Don't Know Where You're Going: Leading in a Liminal Season.* Lanham, MD: Rowman & Littlefield Publishing Group, Inc., 2019.

Brown, Michael Jacoby. *Building Powerful Community Organizations: A Personal Guide to Creating Groups That Can Solve Problems and Change the World.* Arlington, MA: Long Haul Press, 2006.

Brown, Raymond E. *An Introduction to the New Testament.* 1st ed. The Anchor Bible Reference Library. New York, NY: Doubleday, 1997.

Burke, John. *Soul Revolution: How Imperfect People Become All God Intended.* Grand Rapids, MI: Zondervan, 2008.

Cawley, Janet R. *Who Is Our Church? Imagining Congregational Identity.* Herndon, VA: Alban Institute, 2006.

Chalke, Steve. *Change Agents: 25 Hard-Learned Lessons in the Art of Getting Things Done.* Grand Rapids, MI: Zondervan, 2007.

Colyer, Elmer M. *How to Read T. F. Torrance: Understanding His Trinitarian & Scientific Theology.* Downers Grove, IL: InterVarsity Press, 2001.

Covey, Stephen R. *Principle-Centered Leadership.* New York, NY: RosettaBooks, 2009. http://site.ebrary.com/id/10643812.

The 8th Habit: From Effectiveness to Greatness. New York, NY: Free Press, 2004.

The Seven Habits of Highly Effective People: Restoring the Character Ethic. 1st Fireside ed. New York, NY: Fireside Book, 1990.

Covey, Stephen R., A. Roger Merrill, and Rebecca R. Merrill. First Things First: To Live, to Love, to Learn, to Leave a Legacy. New York, NY: Simon & Schuster, 1994.

Crabtree, J. Russell. *Owl Sight: Evidence-Based Discernment and the Promise of Organizational Intelligence for Ministry.* 2012.

Dotson, Junius B. *Developing an Intentional Discipleship System: A Guide for Congregations. See All The People.* Nashville, TN: Discipleship Ministries, 2017.

Goldstein, E. Bruce, ed. *Encyclopedia of Perception.* Los Angeles, CA: SAGE, 2010.

Harney, Kevin. *Leadership from the Inside Out: Examining the Inner Life of a Healthy Church Leader. The Leadership Network Innovation Series.* Grand Rapids, MI: Zondervan, 2007.

Heifetz, Ronald A., and Martin Linsky. *Leadership on the Line: Staying Alive through the Dangers of Leading.* Boston, MA: Harvard Business School Press, 2002.

Marquet, L. David. *Turn the Ship Around! A True Story of Turning Followers into Leaders.* New York, NY: Portfolio, 2012.

Maynard, Phil. *Shift 2: Helping Congregations Come Back into the Game of Effective Ministry.* 2019.

McGriff, E. Carver, and M. Kent Millard. *The Passion Driven Congregation.* Nashville, TN: Abingdon Press, 2003.

Rendle, Gilbert R. Quietly Courageous: *Leading the Church in a Changing World.* Lanham, MD: Rowman & Littlefield, 2019.

Roberts, James A. *Too Much of a Good Thing: Are You Addicted to Your Smartphone?* 2016.

Ruffle, Douglas. *A Missionary Mindset: What Church Leaders Need to Know to Reach Their Community--Lessons from E. Stanley Jones.* Nashville, TN: Discipleship Resources, 2016.

Scharmer, Claus Otto. *Theory U: Leading from the Future as It Emerges.* San Francisco, CA: Berrett-Koehler, 2009.

Sinek, Simon. *Find Your Why: A Practical Guide to Discovering Purpose for You or Your Team.* New York, NY: Portfolio/Penguin, 2017.

Slaughter, Michael. *Momentum for Life: Biblical Principles for Sustaining Physical Health, Personal Integrity, and Strategic Focus.* Rev. ed. Nashville, TN: Abingdon Press, 2008.

Stevens, R. Paul, and Phil Collins. *The Equipping Pastor: A Systems Approach to Congregational Leadership.* Washington, DC: Alban Institute, 1993.

Warren, Richard. *The Purpose Driven Church: Growth without Compromising Your Message & Mission.* Grand Rapids, MI: Zondervan, 1995.

Watson, David Lowes. *Covenant Discipleship: Christian Formation Through Mutual Accountability.* Eugene, OR: Wipf and Stock Publishers, 1998.

Watson, Kevin M., and Scott Thomas Kisker. *The Band Meeting: Rediscovering Relational Discipleship in Transformational Community.* 2017.

Weems, Lovett H. *Church Leadership: Vision, Team, Culture, and Integrity.* Nashville, TN: Abingdon Press, 1993.

Wheatley, Margaret J. *Leadership and the New Science: Discovering Order in a Chaotic World.* 3rd ed. San Francisco, CA: Berrett-Koehler Publishers, Inc., 2006.

What is *The Greatest Expedition*?

The Greatest Expedition is a congregational journey for churches, charges, or cooperative parishes led by a church Expedition Team of 8-12 brave pioneering leaders. The purpose of *The Greatest Expedition* is to provide an experience for Expedition Teams to explore their local context in new ways to develop new MAPS (ministry action plans) so you are more relevant and contextual to reach new people in your community. Updated tools and guides are provided for the church's Expedition Team. Yet, it is a "choose your own adventure" type of journey.

The tools and guides will be provided, but it is up to the church's Expedition Team to decide which tools are needed, which tools just need sharpening, which tools can stay in their backpack to use at a later time, what pathways to explore, and what pathways to pass.

the greatest
EXPEDITION

The Greatest Expedition provides a new lens and updated tools to help your Expedition Team explore and think about being the church in different ways. Will your Expedition Team need to clear the overgrown brush from a once known trail, but not recently traveled? Or will the Expedition Team need to cut a brand new trail with their new tools? Or perhaps, will the Team decide they need to move to a completely fresh terrain and begin breaking ground for something brand new in a foreign climate?

Registration is open and Expedition Teams are launching!

greatestexpedition.com

the greatest
EXPEDITION

These Books Now Available
as resources of
The Greatest Expedition

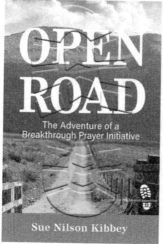

marketsquarebooks.com

These Books Now Available
as resources of
The Greatest Expedition

EXPANDING THE EXPEDITION

through Church Partnerships

CHRISTIAN COON

the greatest EXPEDITION

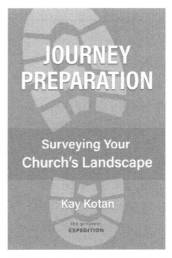

JOURNEY PREPARATION

Surveying Your Church's Landscape

Kay Kotan

the greatest EXPEDITION

the greatest EXPEDITION

A New Kind of Venture Leader

Olu Brown

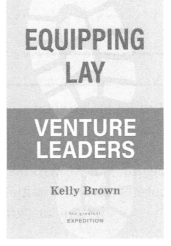

EQUIPPING LAY VENTURE LEADERS

Kelly Brown

the greatest EXPEDITION

Quotes From Other Books
in The Greatest Expedition Series

The multi-site movement keeps the church centered on God's consistent call to go and make disciples for the transformation of the world while staying connected to one another in community.

Ken Nash
Multi-Site Ministry

Stay flexible even when it is not easy. Due to the stress and responsibility of ministry, we can become rigid, pessimistic and fail to see the opportunities in front of us. A mark of great leadership is flexibility, being able to make adjustments when necessary.

Olu Brown
New Kind of Venture Leader

But let me be clear, we will not be making the case that online relationships and connections are the same as in-person ones; we all know they are not. But we will be talking about why online connections are valuable, and there is nothing "virtual" or "almost" about them.

Nicole Reilley
Digital Ministry

Quotes From Other Books
in The Greatest Expedition Series

While we find struggling churches in different contexts, theological backgrounds, sizes, and cultures, declining congregations have one thing in common: There is a palpable lack of focus on what God desires.

Jaye Johnson
Missional Accountability

How you think of your church will determine not only your priorities, but also your energy investment and actions. It will define how you lead and to what extent you live into what the church of Jesus Christ is intended to be.

Sue Nilson Kibbey
Open Road

Any collaboration with local people is a good thing – but the best collaboration is spiritual. It is where we begin to pray together about the community, and the emerging ministry. In such a spiritual collaboration, amazing things begin to happen.

Paul Nixon
Cultural Competency

Now is the time for your church to join us on...

The Greatest Expedition

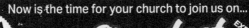

GREATESTEXPEDITION.COM

Nineteen leaders you know and trust have been working more than a year to create 23 books, leadership materials, expedition maps, and events for local congregations, districts, conferences and other groups.

SUE NILSON KIBBEY
Breakthrough Prayer

PHIL MAYNARD
Venture Preparation

KAY KOTAN
Assessing the Current Venture

PAUL NIXON
Cultural Competency

OLU BROWN
A New Kind of Venture Leader

KELLY BROWN
Equipping Lay Venture Leaders

JAYE JOHNSON
Expedition Accountability

KEN WILLARD
The What, Why and Where of the New Expedition

KENDA CREASY-DEAN
Expanding the Expedition Through Social Innovation

DAN JACKSON
Generative Leadership

BLAKE BRADFORD
Strengthening Decision-Making and Governance

CHRISTIAN COON
Evangelizing the Christian

JASON MACKEY
Intentionality & Relationship Building

MILES WELCH
Creating and Sustaining a Traveling Expedition

DAN PEZET
Community Connection

RACHEL GILMORE
Missional Communities

KEN NASH
Expanding the Expedition through Multi-Sites

WAYNE SCHMIDT
Marketplace Multipliers

NICOLE REILLEY
Expanding the Expedition through Digital Ministry

greatestexpedition.com

Visit us on Facebook at:
facebook.com/GreatestExpedition

Market Square

Made in the USA
Middletown, DE
01 June 2023